Instant Redis Optimization How-to

Learn how to tune and optimize Redis for high performance

Arun Chinnachamy

PUBLISHING

BIRMINGHAM - MUMBAI

Instant Redis Optimization How-to

First published: May 2013

Production Reference: 1170513

Published by Packt Publishing Ltd.
Livery Place
35 Livery Street
Birmingham B3 2PB, UK.

ISBN 978-1-78216-480-7

www.packtpub.com

Credits

Author

Arun Chinnachamy

Reviewer

Andrea Pavoni

Acquisition Editor

Andrew Duckworth

Commissioning Editor

Ameya Sawant

Technical Editor

Jeeten Handu

Copy Editors

Aditya Nair

Insiya Morviwala

Project Coordinator

Sherin Padayatty

Proofreader

Kevin McGowan

Graphics

Abhinash Sahu

Production Coordinator

Prachali Bhiwandkar

Cover Work

Prachali Bhiwandkar

Cover Image

Conidon Miranda

About the Author

Arun Chinnachamy is a developer and systems architect who focuses on building scalable web applications, with a degree in Chemical Engineering. He is a multifaceted programmer with experience in multiple technologies and programming languages ranging from ADA to C# over the years.

Currently he leads the technology team at MySmartPrice, one of the leading price comparison engines in India.

I would like to express my gratitude to the great minds that created Redis and made this exciting piece of software open source.

This work would not have been possible without the support of my parents and my wife, Suvarchala, who was patient with my round-the-clock working hours.

Thanks to Sitakanta and Sulakshan for introducing me to MySmartPrice and providing me with an opportunity to work there; MySmartPrice started my love affair with Redis.

I would like to thank the open source community for excellent documentation about Redis; it was of incredible help during my early days with Redis.

It is totally unfair to not thank my editor and publisher who believed in me and provided me with this excellent opportunity to share my experience with you.

I would also like to thank each and every one who shaped my career over the years and helped me find the best in me.

About the Reviewer

Andrea Pavoni is a passionate Italian programmer. He's mostly focused on web and mobile development, always looking for the best tools available. Andrea is also an active member of the Italian Ruby community. He helped in the organization for Ruby Day (2011-2012) and coached at the first Italian Rails Girls event in Rome.

www.PacktPub.com

Support files, eBooks, discount offers and more

You might want to visit www.PacktPub.com for support files and downloads related to your book.

Did you know that Packt offers eBook versions of every book published, with PDF and ePub files available? You can upgrade to the eBook version at www.PacktPub.com and as a print book customer, you are entitled to a discount on the eBook copy. Get in touch with us at service@packtpub.com for more details.

At www.PacktPub.com, you can also read a collection of free technical articles, sign up for a range of free newsletters and receive exclusive discounts and offers on Packt books and eBooks.

http://PacktLib.PacktPub.com

Do you need instant solutions to your IT questions? PacktLib is Packt's online digital book library. Here, you can access, read and search across Packt's entire library of books.

Why Subscribe?

- ▶ Fully searchable across every book published by Packt
- ▶ Copy and paste, print and bookmark content
- ▶ On demand and accessible via web browser

Free Access for Packt account holders

If you have an account with Packt at www.PacktPub.com, you can use this to access PacktLib today and view nine entirely free books. Simply use your login credentials for immediate access.

Table of Contents

Preface

The computing world is changing fast. In this fast-moving world, the only way to survive is to deliver data quickly. We are moving towards a world in which even a second counts and can affect user behavior drastically. That is why the whole NoSQL movement started. NoSQL data stores were able to provide faster access by sacrificing some of the advantages that traditional databases offer. Redis is one of the fastest data stores in the market and is being used by many giants in the web industry.

It is important for software professionals to keep up-to-date with the latest technology offerings and tools in the market, which is critical to gain advantage in business. The main goal of this book is to introduce you to Redis. The book helps you to understand the various configurations and options available in Redis, which could ease your efforts of adding Redis to your application stack.

What this book covers

Choosing your data store (Simple) shows what data store to select from top names like Cassandra, MongoDB, Riak, CouchBase, MemCached, and others, based on your application requirements.

Installing Redis (Simple) focuses on a step-by-step installation procedure of Redis in Linux systems, with commands to test the installation.

Configuring and tuning Redis (Intermediate) helps you understand all configurations available in Redis and how to effectively configure the server to make the most out of it.

Implementing persistence in Redis (Intermediate) defines all the options available in Redis to enable data persistence. You can choose the options based on the data durability you prefer.

Detecting performance bottlenecks (Intermediate) helps you understand the various bottlenecks in Redis and how effectively you can mitigate them to make the most out of your installation.

Performing high-volume writes (Advanced) tells you about high-volume writes into Redis. It helps you to load a large amount of data in very little time, either through pipelining or using the Redis protocol.

Leveraging data types (Simple) helps you understand the most important feature in Redis—data types. This recipe helps you understand the data types and how to use them to create even more complex data types.

Optimizing memory (Intermediate) helps you reach the goal of optimizing the memory usage of this in-memory data store. It explains presharding and how to use the auto-expiry feature in Redis with a real-life example.

Using transactions and Pub/Sub (Advanced) covers one of the advanced features in Redis, which makes it an ideal broadcast for servers. This also helps you understand transactions and how to use Publish/Subscribe in Redis with a real-life example of a messaging system.

Troubleshooting and monitoring (Intermediate) tells you about debugging and monitoring the installation using the Slow log or `monitor` command in Redis. This recipe also explains how to use the Redis watchdog to diagnose software bugs.

Using languages and drivers (Simple) helps you choose a driver library to communicate with Redis using your favorite language.

What you need for this book

In order to make your learning more efficient, you need a computer with any flavor of Linux, preferably Ubuntu or Debian, installed. Redis is not production-ready in Windows, but you can check the *Installing Redis (Simple)* recipe for ports of Redis in Windows.

Also, you need an Internet connection to the machine to download the latest source of Redis from the repository. You also need a text editor you are comfortable with in order to edit the Redis configuration files.

Who this book is for

This book is for developers and/or system administrators who are already proficient in programming and traditional database systems and want to learn about Redis for its simplicity and fast performance. If you are a developer, it is also expected that you have proficiency in at least one programming language through which you want to communicate with Redis.

Conventions

In this book, you will find a number of styles of text that distinguish between different kinds of information. Here are some examples of these styles, and an explanation of their meaning.

Code words in text are shown as follows:

"One of the limits you might want to set is `maxclients`, which controls how many clients can connect to the server simultaneously."

Any command-line input or output is written as follows:

```
$<numberofbytesofargumentN>CRLF
<argumentdata>CRLF
```

New terms and **important words** are shown in bold. Words that you see on the screen, in menus or dialog boxes for example, appear in the text like this: "To solve this particular problem, Redis provides another way of persistence, **Append-only file (AOF)**".

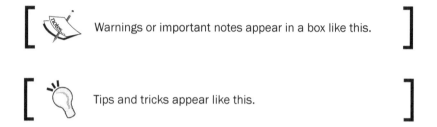

Warnings or important notes appear in a box like this.

Tips and tricks appear like this.

Reader feedback

Feedback from our readers is always welcome. Let us know what you think about this book—what you liked or may have disliked. Reader feedback is important for us to develop titles that you really get the most out of.

To send us general feedback, simply send an e-mail to `feedback@packtpub.com`, and mention the book title via the subject of your message.

If there is a topic that you have expertise in and you are interested in either writing or contributing to a book, see our author guide on `www.packtpub.com/authors`.

Customer support

Now that you are the proud owner of a Packt book, we have a number of things to help you to get the most from your purchase.

Downloading the example code

You can download the example code files for all Packt books you have purchased from your account at `http://www.packtpub.com`. If you purchased this book elsewhere, you can visit `http://www.packtpub.com/support` and register to have the files e-mailed directly to you.

Errata

Although we have taken every care to ensure the accuracy of our content, mistakes do happen. If you find a mistake in one of our books—maybe a mistake in the text or the code—we would be grateful if you would report this to us. By doing so, you can save other readers from frustration and help us improve subsequent versions of this book. If you find any errata, please report them by visiting http://www.packtpub.com/submit-errata, selecting your book, clicking on the **erratasubmissionform** link, and entering the details of your errata. Once your errata are verified, your submission will be accepted and the errata will be uploaded on our website, or added to any list of existing errata, under the Errata section of that title. Any existing errata can be viewed by selecting your title from http://www.packtpub.com/support.

Piracy

Piracy of copyright material on the Internet is an ongoing problem across all media. At Packt, we take the protection of our copyright and licenses very seriously. If you come across any illegal copies of our works, in any form, on the Internet, please provide us with the location address or website name immediately so that we can pursue a remedy.

Please contact us at copyright@packtpub.com with a link to the suspected pirated material.

We appreciate your help in protecting our authors, and our ability to bring you valuable content.

Questions

You can contact us at questions@packtpub.com if you are having a problem with any aspect of the book, and we will do our best to address it.

Instant Redis Optimization How-to

Welcome to *Instant Redis Optimization How-to*. In this book, we are going to discuss what Redis is, and how to install, optimize, and leverage this ultrafast NoSQL database server. This book provides in-depth insight into how and where to add Redis to your application stack.

Choosing your data store (Simple)

Every database software is written to solve a specific problem and is best suited to that. It takes a lot of hard work to select a data store that fits your application requirements. It is always important to pick the right tool for the right job. In this recipe, we will see which data store to select from top names like Cassandra, MongoDB, Riak, CouchBase, MemCached, and others, based on your application requirements.

Getting ready

First, we will learn about Redis and why it was created, before we look into other data stores available. Redis is an advanced open source key-value store that is capable of storing data structures like strings, lists, hashes, and sets. Redis, which means REmote DIctionary Server, is an in-memory database in which the whole data set needs to be available in the memory during runtime. It supports persistence by dumping the dataset as a file on the disk or by appending every command as a log. This single-threaded application is written in ANSI-C and the server leaves very little memory footprint. Another plus point is that Redis provides a very simple client protocol, which is similar to Telnet.

It is important we know the reason why Redis was created and how it scales when compared to other similar offerings.

Why was Redis created?

Redis was started by Salvatore Sanfilippo to improve and extend LLOOGG, which is a real-time website-analytics system. Once Redis became stable enough for production environments and grew in popularity, it turned into a standalone open source project under BSD license, completely sponsored by VMware.

Who is using Redis?

If you are a social or a technology person, you have undoubtedly experienced the fast performance of Redis. For example, Quora uses Redis to provide the front-page feeds and Twitter implements Redis for its deep-structured awareness. The list goes on with high-profile online applications such as GitHub, Stack OverFlow, YouPorn, and Craigslist,.

How to do it...

- ▶ If your data is structured, predictable, and relational, it is best to use relational databases like Oracle, MySQL, or MSSQL
- ▶ In the case of document-oriented records with the functionality to perform range queries, indexing, and MapReduce, check out MongoDB or a similar document database
- ▶ If you are dealing with occasional data changes and want to run predefined queries on it, CouchBase fits in nicely
- ▶ If you need single-site fault tolerance, scalability, and dynamo-like data storage, Riak is your option
- ▶ If you are looking for a simple cache with less support of data types and better expiry algorithms, MemCached is the better choice
- ▶ Redis was built to work with highly dynamic and nonstructured data with support for complex data types

There's more...

Redis is not an alternative to relational databases like MSSQL, Oracle, or MySQL. If your data is highly dynamic and updated often, managing the relational database tends to be a difficult task. Redis fits into this perfectly.

- ▶ Redis serves as an excellent cache server—commonly referred to as "MemCached on steroids".
- ▶ Redis is well suited in situations where performance is critical and the data set changes very often. This makes it perfect for leader boards and a statistics tracker.
- ▶ Due to its Pub/Sub support, Redis can be effectively used as a multiprocess communication queue.
- ▶ Redis can be used as reliable queues by taking advantage of atomic operations on lists.

If you are looking to use Redis as your primary database, you can check out `moot.it`, which is using Redis as its primary database and has attained incredible results (`https://moot. it/blog/technology/redis-as-primary-datastore-wtf.html`).

How does Redis compare with the competition?

It is important to know what we can do with Redis and it is equally important to know how it compares with other similar offerings in the market. So, in this section, we will learn how it varies in general and compare it with a few important NoSQL data stores.

Major differences

In general, let's see how Redis compares with other NoSQL databases and what it provides that makes it stand out from the group.

▶ It supports more complex data structures when compared to other stores. It natively supports many fundamental data types, providing a rich set of primitives for manipulation of data.

▶ Redis supports atomic operations on its data types through low-level APIs.

▶ Being an in-memory database, Redis provides atomic operations with little internal complexity.

▶ It has a low memory footprint of about 1 MB for an instance. The memory required by Redis to store overhead information such as type information and reference count, becomes trivial when compared to the stored data.

▶ Redis is ACID-compliant (Atomicity, Consistency, Isolation, and Durability). Other NoSQL databases are not or are partially ACID-compliant.

Comparison with other data stores

Redis is one of the very few databases in which you can predict the time complexity for any operation. The server is being developed with performance in its DNA. So let us have a look at how it compares with other similar offerings in the NoSQL space.

▶ **MongoDB** (`http://www.mongodb.org/`): Both MongoDB and Redis are built to serve different purposes and to solve different problems in traditional relational database systems. They are both popular and work well together. MongoDB is used to store persistent data whereas Redis can be used for temporary data for faster access.

▶ **Cassandra** (`https://cassandra.apache.org/`): Cassandra is more optimized for write operations than read operation. An application that does more writes, such as logging systems, can take full advantage of Cassandra. It was built to manage data which cannot be held in a single server, whereas Redis is built to keep all the data in the memory of a single server.

▶ **Riak** (`http://basho.com/riak/`): If you want to store dynamo-like data and are looking for no downtime, Riak is the best option. It is a very good fault-tolerant and scalable single-site data storage engine with MapReduce support.

> ▶ **MemCached** (`http://www.memcached.org/`): While MongoDB is trying to replace relational databases, Redis is trying to do the same to the other end of the spectrum, MemCached. Redis performs better than MemCached in many benchmarks and can be easily validated using the **redis-benchmark** application, which comes along with the installation. The important and critical differences between MemCached and Redis are:

> - ❑ Support for replication in Redis.
> - ❑ Missing persistence support in MemCached. Even though there is a chance of losing some data in Redis, losing a small chunk of data is better than losing everything on server failure or restart.
> - ❑ Support for a rich set of data types in Redis.

Installing Redis (Simple)

Before we start learning about Redis and how we can leverage on its fast performance, we need to install and have a working server. The installation of Redis is easy and straightforward.

Getting ready

In order to install, we need a computer system with a working Linux environment or a Mac OS X. If using Linux, I assume you have installed the Debian or Ubuntu operating system for this book. For the other operating system, you can refer to the *There's more* section of this recipe. As the Debian or Ubuntu packages are usually outdated, we will see how to install the Redis server from the source. Make sure you are using the latest stable version, as Redis is under active development and new commands and improvements pop out in every version. There are no dependencies for the Redis server except `libc`, which will be available in your system by default. But to build the server from the source, you need the compiler.

How to do it...

1. We will start with installing the build tools which are necessary to build Redis from the source. Open the terminal program and execute the following command:

   ```
   # sudo apt-get update
   ```

2. Once the command executes, download the compiler with build essentials, which is a package of all the common build tools to build the Redis server from the source.

   ```
   # sudo apt-get install build-essential
   ```

3. Now we have all the components to build the source. The following URL always has the latest stable build (2.6.13), which eliminates the confusion of version numbers:

```
# wget http://download.redis.io/redis-stable.tar.gz
# tar xvzf redis-stable.tar.gz
# cd redis-stable
# make
# sudo make install
```

How it works...

Building a Redis server from the source is easy and it gets the latest version. The preceding steps will download the latest version of Redis from the repository, compile the C source, and install them in the machine. In this section, we will understand about various executables generated in this process.

You can install any unstable builds using the same procedure.

Caution

Be aware that the unstable builds usually have bugs and are not for production environments, so do not use them unless you are sure about what you are doing.

On successful execution of the preceding procedure, the following binaries are built from the source:

- ▶ **redis-server**: The server executable
- ▶ **redis-cli**: The command-line interface for working with the Redis server
- ▶ **redis-benchmark**: For performance benchmarking and to test your setup
- ▶ **redis-check-aof**: For debugging corrupt data files
- ▶ **redis-check-dump**: For debugging corrupt data files

There's more...

Now that we have built the Redis binaries from the source, we will see how to set up the Redis server with configuration files and test the installation.

Setting up and testing

The `make install` command copies all the executables to the `/usr/local/bin` folder. The configuration files and init scripts are not yet in place to run Redis.

1. You can run the `install_server.sh` script, which can be found inside the `utils` folder of the Redis source. In the terminal, go to the `utils` folder inside `redis-stable` and execute the following command:

   ```
   # ./install_server.sh
   ```

2. The script will produce a series of questions about the path to where the configuration files are to be kept. If you are not sure, just press the *Enter* key (*Return*) to keep the default value. Once the installation is completed, the Redis server will be started by the script.

3. Now the server is running with the configuration available in the file `/etc/redis/6379.conf`. Run `redis-cli` to test the server in another terminal window.

   ```
   # redis-cli
   ```

4. If the Redis server is installed and is running, the prompt will look something like this:

   ```
   redis 127.0.0.1:6379>
   ```

5. You can issue a couple of commands to get the feel of working with the Redis server:

   ```
   SET Android Google
   SET Windows Microsoft
   SET iOS Apple
   ```

6. The preceding commands will create keys of type `string` (Android, Windows, and iOS) and set their values to their respective company names. To check the server, issue the `GET` command using the keys created to retrieve their values.

   ```
   GET Android
   Google
   GET iOS
   Apple
   QUIT
   ```

7. The `QUIT` command closes the connection from the server. To stop the server, issue the following command. Using `shutdown` makes sure that Redis saves the data to the disk before quitting gracefully.

   ```
   # redis-cli shutdown
   ```

Now we have a working Redis server with the basic configuration.

Redis in Mac OS X

If you are using Mac OS X, you can install Redis from the source or by using Homebrew. The installation process from the source is the same as we did for Debian. So we will see how to install Redis in Mac using Homebrew. You should have OS X command-line tools installed in the system for Homebrew to work. If you do not have the command-line tools installed, you can download them from the Apple Developer website (`http://connect.apple.com/`).

1. To install Homebrew, execute the following command in the terminal:

   ```
   ruby <(curl -fsSk https://raw.github.com/mxcl/homebrew/go)
   ```

2. To check the successful installation of Homebrew, run the following command:

   ```
   brew doctor
   ```

3. You are one step away from installing Redis. Execute the following command:

   ```
   brew install redis
   ```

Homebrew installs and configures the server. You can test the installation by running `redis-cli` and issuing commands to the server.

Redis in Windows

If you are a loyal user of the Windows operating system, you have hit a hurdle. Unfortunately, Redis is not officially supported in Windows 32- or 64-bit systems. But there are various ports available that are not of production quality and can be used only for development purposes. As Redis is not natively supported in Windows, the performance of ported builds is not even close to its performance in Linux. But if you do not have access to Linux systems, the compiled packages can be downloaded from the GitHub page of the officially recommended Windows port (`https://github.com/dmajkic/redis/downloads`).

As it is not officially supported for Windows, the book will focus on the Linux installation, and using a Linux system is strongly recommended.

Configuring and tuning Redis (Intermediate)

Redis is highly configurable and exposes all the configuration parameters through a file that should be passed as a parameter to the server executable. In our previous recipe, we used the configuration file placed at the path `/etc/redis/6379.conf`. The configuration options available in Redis are extensive. Let us take a look at what the options are to use these files and how to tune the server for maximum performance. Data persistence in Redis and various other options of persistence are explained in the next recipe in detail. In this section, let us see how to configure the network and security in Redis.

Getting ready

To start configuring, open the file in the path `/etc/redis/6379.conf` in your favourite editor, be it VIM, Emacs, GEdit, or Nano. After changing and saving any configuration, Redis needs to be restarted for the changes to take effect.

How to do it...

1. The first and foremost configuration is to daemonize the server. Look for `daemonize no` and change it to `daemonize yes`. By default, Redis listens to all network interfaces. If you want to connect to Redis only from a local system and do not want to connect from other computers in the network, you can uncomment the following line:

    ```
    bind 127.0.0.1
    ```

2. The next important configuration that you may want in the production environment is `timeout`. This configuration defines the time after which the idle connection with a client will be closed.

    ```
    timeout 20
    ```

3. Redis logs provide important information about the server operations. Set the `loglevel` attribute to `notice` in the production environment to prevent the bloating of the logfile.

    ```
    loglevel notice
    ```

4. By default, `log` is piped to the standard output. As we have daemonized the process, the logs will vanish into the black hole (`/dev/null`). In order to store the logfile, replace `logfile stdout` with `logfile /var/log/redis.log`.

5. If you do not want another log file, you can manage the logs using the system logger by setting the value of `syslog-enabled` to yes.

6. Another important configuration is `databases`. This parameter defines how many databases are allowed in the current instance of Redis. The default value is `16`. If you want to have more databases, change the number appropriately. The database ID is zero-based. In the case of 16 databases, the database ID starts from `0` and ranges up to `15`.

    ```
    databases 16
    ```

7. Slow log is a feature that logs the queries or operations that take more than the configured execution time. Slow Logs help in debugging the queries that cause performance issues.

    ```
    slowlog-log-slower-than 10000
    ```

8. The Slow log feature consumes memory. When the newest slow query is logged, the oldest one is removed if the maximum length of the Slow log is reached.

    ```
    slowlog-max-len 128
    ```

How it works...

By default, Redis starts as a foreground process and stuffs the terminal window with the server output. So it is important to run Redis as a background process. The `timeout` parameter helps the server by terminating idle connections when clients make connections and forgot to close them. Set this to some reasonable time period (in seconds) based on the operations you might perform with the server. Set this to `0` to disable the timeout. The configuration parameters in this file control Redis and its behaviour.

There's more...

By default, Redis uses port 6379 for listening to clients. If you want to change the port number, you can change the port to an appropriate value. For the context of this book, default port 6379 is assumed.

Security settings

Security comes into picture only when Redis is connected to the systems through the network. When you want the clients to connect to Redis from external systems, you need to take extra measures to make sure your data is safe and cannot be exploited. If there is no authentication to the Redis instance, it is very easy to clear the entire data using a single command. In order to prevent this, Redis provides an authentication mechanism using a password.

Uncomment the line that starts with `requirepass` and replace the word next to it with a strong password. As mentioned in the configuration file, it is very easy to break a simple password using brute force due to the sheer speed of Redis.

```
requirepass reD1$$er\/erR0ck$
```

Another security feature provided by Redis is command renaming. For an authenticated client, it is easy to change the configuration of the server using the `CONFIG` command. To prevent any misuse of commands and to restrict clients from using certain commands, you can use the command-renaming option.

For instance, if you see the command in the configuration file, then the `CONFIG` command can be renamed to some random sequence—preventing any clients, except internal tools, from using the command.

```
rename-command CONFIG b840fc02d524045429941cc15f59e41cb7be6c52
```

You can also kill any command completely by just renaming the command to an empty string.

One of the limits you might want to set is `maxclients`, which controls how many clients can connect to the server simultaneously. After reaching the maximum connections, the new connections will be ignored. So, set this with caution after considering your use case. This parameter, along with `timeout`, can be used to limit and control the client's connection to the server.

```
maxclients 100
```

 If you are going to use Redis as a caching server, consider using `maxmemory`, which limits the amount of memory Redis can utilize.

Advanced configuration

Redis encodes the data types into more efficient data structures to optimize the memory space when the size of data in the memory is less than the configured limit. Data types like hashes, lists, sets made of integers, and sorted sets with size less than the configured element size are encoded in an efficient way that uses up to 10 times lesser memory. This is completely transparent to the clients that are performing the operations and can be controlled using the configuration parameters. Redis performs the operation of converting these special encoded types to normal data structures as soon as the data size exceeds the configured value, in a completely transparent manner.

Let us leave the configuration to default. We will discuss how these work and what the significance of these numbers is, in the *Optimizing memory* recipe.

Implementing persistence in Redis (Intermediate)

Persistence is important and is one of the critical features for any database. The expectation from any data store is to have no data loss on server failure and have a fully durable copy of the data in the disk. Almost every NoSQL database has trouble with this, and Redis is no exception.

Getting ready

Redis provides configuration settings for persistence and for enabling durability of data depending on the project statement.

> ▸ If durability of data is critical
> ▸ If durability of data is not important

You can achieve persistence of data using the snapshotting mode, which is the simplest mode in Redis. Depending on the configuration, Redis saves a dump of all the data sets in its memory into a single RDB file. The interval in which Redis dumps the memory can be configured to happen every X seconds or after Y operations. Consider an example of a moderately busy server that receives 15,000 changes every minute over its 1 GB data set in memory. Based on the snapshotting rule, the data will be stored every 60 seconds or whenever there are at least 15,000 writes. So the snapshotting runs every minute and writes the entire data of 1 GB to the disk, which soon turns ugly and very inefficient.

To solve this particular problem, Redis provides another way of persistence, **Append-only file** (**AOF**), which is the main persistence option in Redis. This is similar to journal files, where all the operations performed are recorded and replayed in the same order to rebuild the exact state.

Redis's AOF persistence supports three different modes:

- ▶ **No fsync**: In this mode, we take a chance and let the operating system decide when to flush the data. This is the fastest of the three modes.

- ▶ **fsync every second**: This mode is a compromised middle point between performance and durability. Data will be flushed using fsync every second. If the disk is not able to match the write speed, the fsync can take more than a second, in which case Redis delays the write up to another second. So this mode guarantees a write to be committed to OS buffers and transferred to the disk within 2 seconds in the worst-case scenario.

- ▶ **fsync always**: This is the last and safest mode. This provides complete durability of data at a heavy cost to performance. In this mode, the data needs to be written to the file and synced with the disk using fsync before the client receives an acknowledgment. This is the slowest of all three modes.

How to do it...

First let us see how to configure snapshotting, followed by the Append-only file method:

1. In Redis, we can configure when a new snapshot of the data set will be performed. For example, Redis can be configured to dump the memory if the last dump was created more than 30 seconds ago and there are at least 100 keys that are modified or created.

2. Snapshotting should be configured in the `/etc/redis/6379.conf` file. The configuration can be as follows:

   ```
   save 900 1
   save 60 10000
   ```

3. The first line translates to take a snapshot of data after 900 seconds if at least one key has changed, while the second line translates to snapshotting every 60 seconds if 10,000 keys have been modified in the meantime.

4. The configuration parameter `rdbcompression` defines whether the RDB file is to be compressed or not. There is a trade-off between the CPU and RDB dump file size.

5. We are interested in changing the dump's filename using the `dbfilename` parameter. Redis uses the current folder to create the dump files. For convenience, it is advised to store the RDB file in a separate folder.

   ```
   dbfilename redis-snapshot.rdb
   dir /var/lib/redis/
   ```

6. Let us run a small test to make sure the RDB dump is working. Start the server again. Connect to the server using `redis-cli`, as we did already. To test whether our snapshotting is working, issue the following commands:

   ```
   SET Key Value
   SAVE
   ```

7. After the `SAVE` command, a file should be created in the folder `/var/lib/redis` with the name `redis-snapshot.rdb`. This confirms that our installation is able to take a snapshot of our data into a file.

Now let us see how to configure persistence in Redis using the AOF method:

1. The configuration for persistence through AOF also goes into the same file located in `/etc/redis/6379.conf`. By default, the Append-only mode is not enabled. Enable it using the `appendonly` parameter.

   ```
   appendonly yes
   ```

2. Also, if you would like to specify a filename for the AOF log, uncomment the line and change the filename.

   ```
   appendfilename redis-aof.aof
   ```

3. The `appendfsync everysec` command provides a good balance between performance and durability.

   ```
   appendfsync everysec
   ```

4. Redis needs to know when it has to rewrite the AOF file. This will be decided based on two configuration parameters, as follows:

   ```
   auto-aof-rewrite-percentage 100
   auto-aof-rewrite-min-size 64mb
   ```

5. Unless the minimum size is reached and the percentage of the increase in size when compared to the last rewrite is less than 100 percent, the AOF rewrite will not be performed.

How it works...

First let us see how snapshotting works.

When one of the criteria is met, Redis forks the process. The child process starts writing the RDB file to the disk at the folder specified in our configuration file. Meanwhile, the parent process continues to serve the requests. The problem with this approach is that the parent process stores the keys, which change during this snapshotting by the child, in the extra memory. In the worst-case scenario, if all the keys are modified, the memory usage spikes to roughly double.

Caution

Be aware that the bigger the RDB file, the longer it takes Redis to restore the data on startup.

Corruption of the RDB file is not possible as it is created by the append-only method from the data in Redis's memory, by the child process. The new RDB file is created as a temporary file and is then renamed to the destination file using the atomic rename system call once the dump is completed.

AOF's working is simple. Every time a write operation is performed, the command operation gets logged into a logfile. The format used in the logfile is the same as the format used by clients to communicate to the server. This helps in easy parsing of AOF files, which brings in the possibility of replaying the operation in another Redis instance. Only the operations that change the data set are written to the log. This log will be used on startup to reconstruct the exact data.

As we are continuously writing the operations into the log, the AOF file explodes in size as compared to the amount of operations performed. So, usually, the size of the AOF file is larger than the RDB dump. Redis manages the increasing size of the data log by compacting the file in a non-blocking manner periodically. For example, say a specific key, key1, has changed 100 times using the SET command. In order to recreate the final state in the last minute, only the last SET command is required. We do not need information about the previous 99 SET commands. This might look simple in theory, but it gets complex when dealing with complex data structures and operations such as union and intersection. Due to this complexity, it becomes very difficult to compress the existing file.

To reduce the complexity of compacting the AOF, Redis starts with the data in the memory and rewrites the AOF file from scratch. This is more similar to the snapshotting method. Redis forks a child process that recreates the AOF file and performs an atomic rename to swap the old file with a new one. The same problem, of the requirement of extra memory for operations performed during the rewrite, is present here. So the memory required can spike up to two times based on the operations while writing an AOF file.

There's more...

Both snapshotting and AOF have their own advantages and limitations, which makes it ideal to use both at the same time. Let us now discuss the major advantages and limitations in the snapshotting method.

Advantages of snapshotting

The advantages of configuring snapshotting in Redis are as follows:

  ▸ RDB is a single compact file that cannot get corrupted due to the way it is created. It is very easy to implement.

  ▸ This dump file is perfect to take backups and for disaster recovery of remote servers. The RDB file can just be copied and saved for future recoveries.

  ▸ In comparison, this approach has little or no influence over performance as the only work the parent process needs to perform is forking a child process. The parent process will never perform any disk operations; they are all performed by the child process.

  ▸ As an RDB file can be compressed, it provides a faster restart when compared to the append-only file method, which is discussed in the next recipe.

Limitations of snapshotting

Snapshotting, in spite of the advantages mentioned, has a few limitations that you should be aware of:

  ▸ The periodic background save can result in significant loss of data in case of server or hardware failure.

  ▸ The `fork()` process used to save the data might take a moment, during which the server will stop serving clients. The larger the data set to be saved, the longer it takes the `fork()` process to complete.

  ▸ The memory needed for the data set might double in the worst-case scenario, when all the keys in the memory are modified while snapshotting is in progress.

What should we use?

Now that we have discussed both the modes of persistence Redis provides us with, the big question is what should we use? The answer to this question is entirely based on our application and requirements. In cases where we expect good durability, both snapshotting and AOF can be turned on and be made to work in unison, providing us with redundant persistence. Redis always restores the data from AOF wherever applicable, as it is supposed to have better durability with little loss of data. Both RDB and AOF files can be copied and stored for future use or for recovering another instance of Redis.

In a few cases, where performance is very critical, memory usage is limited, and persistence is also paramount, persistence can be turned off completely. In these cases, replication can be used to get durability. Replication is a process in which two Redis instances, one master and one slave, are in sync with the same data. Clients are served by the master, and the master server syncs the data with a slave.

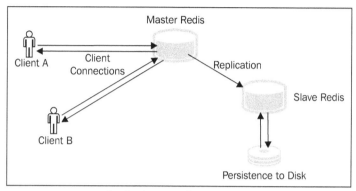

Replication setup for persistence

Consider a setup as shown in the preceding image; that is:

▶ Master instance with no persistence

▶ Slave instance with AOF enabled

In this case, the master does not need to perform any background disk operations and is fully dedicated to serve client requests, except for a trivial slave connection. The slave server configured with AOF performs the disk operations. As mentioned before, this file can be used to restore the master in case of a disaster.

Persistence in Redis is a matter of configuration, balancing the trade-off between performance, disk I/O, and data durability. If you are looking for more information on persistence in Redis, you will find the article by Salvatore Sanfilippo at `http://oldblog.antirez.com/post/redis-persistence-demystified.html` interesting.

Detecting performance bottlenecks (Intermediate)

Redis is now well known for its performance. However, its performance depends not only on the server but is also influenced by the environment in which it is running. There are various factors that could affect the performance of Redis. The factors range from server setup and hardware to memory management by the operating system. In this recipe, let us discuss a few things that are to be considered to get the maximum out of Redis.

Getting ready

The major bottlenecks that need to be considered are:

- ▸ Network and communication
- ▸ RAM
- ▸ I/O operations

By considering the guidelines that follow, we can reduce these latencies and get better performance from the Redis instance.

How to do it...

- ▸ Use Unix domain sockets for clients connecting from a local host.
- ▸ Use command pipelining whenever possible. More information about pipelining will be provided in the next recipe.
- ▸ Avoid using virtual instances for running Redis. Always run Redis in a physical machine to get better performance.
- ▸ Always make sure we have enough RAM to accommodate the whole data set and the spikes, during save operations. Avoid data overflowing into the swap partition.
- ▸ Consider using faster disk I/O devices for saving RDB and AOF files.
- ▸ As the connections to the server are TCP-based, in order to reduce overhead, it is advised to keep the connection open as long as possible rather than opening and closing connections multiple times from the same script.
- ▸ It is advised to dedicate a CPU core to a Redis instance; but if it is not configured correctly, it could lead to bad performance.

How it works...

In most scenarios, the clients will connect to the Redis instance over a network through a TCP/IP connection. So, the total time taken for a request to complete is calculated by:

Total time for request completion = network latency to reach server + time taken by Redis to process and respond + network latency for response to come back

Even if Redis can process in a few microseconds, the low performance will be recorded because of the multiple roundtrips made to the Redis server. For example, let us consider that two clients are connecting to the same Redis server. One of the clients is connecting from a remote system from where an average roundtrip takes around 150 ms, and another client is connecting to the server from the local host through the Unix domain socket. Assume that in both cases Redis can complete the operation in 2 ms tops.

For the first client, the time taken to perform 1,000 individual commands will be:

Time taken = 1000 x (100 ms + 2 ms) = 102000 ms = 102 seconds.

For the second client, which is connecting from a local host, the latency can be as low as 30 microseconds, or in the worst-case scenario, say, 100 microseconds.

Time taken = 1000 x (100 microseconds + 2 ms) = 2100 ms = 2.1 seconds.

So, the longer it takes a request to reach the server, the longer it takes to complete the request. Apart from the network latency, more latency is added by the operating system for packet queuing. The latency gets aggravated in the case of virtual machines when compared to the physical machines, due to the extra level of networking.

So by using sockets, pipelining commands, and reducing networking layers, we can achieve better performance from the same Redis instance.

As mentioned earlier, Redis needs to keep the complete data set in the memory to work. In the case of larger data sets, it is common for the system to run out of physical RAM when lots of other processes are also running on the same machine. To free some physical RAM, the server will start swapping.

 Paging is a memory-management scheme that allows the operating system to use the disk as a swap or secondary memory when the RAM cannot hold all the data. This virtual memory implementation is important for the working of all operating systems.

To make room for other processes in the RAM, the operating system swaps the memory block between the physical disk and RAM. In case the system is running out of physical memory, it takes the memory block of Redis and swaps it to the disk. When Redis needs to access that specific memory block, the server needs to swap the paging file back to the physical RAM before Redis can access it. When this happens, Redis's performance goes down drastically. To prevent this, keep monitoring the RAM usage of Redis and install two times more RAM than the size of the data set.

 Consider using the `maxmemory` option to limit the amount of RAM used for caching purposes.

Persistence is not perfect in Redis and it comes with a few drawbacks of its own. As discussed in the previous recipe, *Persistence in Redis*, both the persistence modes in Redis, Snapshotting and AOF, have to fork a child process to generate an RDB file and rewrite an AOF file respectively. Redis uses copy-on-write forking, letting both parent and child processes share the common memory pages. The memory pages are duplicated only when any change happens in the parent or child process. As the fork operation is initiated by a parent process, it could cause some latency. If the disk resources are shared with other processes and if any other process is performing disk I/O, the performance can deteriorate considerably.

If the AOF is configured with **fsync always**, it will create more disk I/Os that in turn translate into more latency in the system. This latency in the disk can be minimized by avoiding other processes performing I/O in the same system.

It is recommended to use **Solid State Disk** (**SSD**) for AOF and RDB files, which helps in decreasing the disk latency, or dedicate a disk only for Redis.

There's more...

Apart from the network, RAM, and disk I/O, there are a couple of other factors that may affect the performance of Redis.

CPU bottleneck

Redis is a single-threaded application. A single thread serves all the requests from the clients. In cases where multiple simultaneous requests are received, the requests are queued and processed sequentially. This might look like a bad idea, as requests may take longer to be processed than expected, but Redis is not perceived as slow due to the very little time taken to complete a single request, and the thread does not get blocked in any I/O operations as all the I/O operations are performed by the forked child processes.

Due to the single-threaded architecture, even when provided with multiple cores, Redis cannot leverage them. So Redis likes processors with larger caches and is neutral towards multiple cores. There is very little chance of the CPU becoming the bottleneck, as Redis is usually memory- or network-bound.

But to make use of multiple cores, we can start multiple Redis instances in the same server using different ports and treating them as different servers. Due to the low memory footprint of Redis (approximately 1 MB per instance), we can run multiple instances without any serious load to the memory.

Latency due to the application's design

Apart from the server setup and persistence, even the application's design can affect the performance of Redis. For example:

- Making Redis write logs at the debug level creates serious performance issues. In the production environment, make sure the log level is set to `notice` or `warning`.

- Slow commands can also affect the performance of Redis. Latency is created by complex commands too. As all the requests in Redis are served using a single thread, any command that takes longer increases the response time for other commands. Though basic commands take very little time, performing sorting, union, or intersection between two large sets will take a while. The `SLOW LOG` command needs to be monitored and optimized.

- Redis provides a mechanism for auto-expiring keys in its data set. When inserting a key, expiry time for the key can also be mentioned. When the expiry time is reached, Redis destroys and flushes the key. An expiry cycle in Redis runs every 100 milliseconds. This needs additional processing to make sure too much memory is not used by keys that are already expired. One of the sources of latency can be too many keys expiring at the same time.

Performing high-volume writes (Advanced)

Redis is known as an ultrafast data store because it can not only deliver data at a higher speed but also accept new data into its data set at a higher speed. There is not much performance difference between read and write operations in Redis, leaving persistence aside. It is critical to know how to feed a large set of data into Redis in a short burst of time.

The write operation in Redis can be of two types:

- Data operations like set, union, increment, or others.

- Bulk data import into Redis. For example, importing millions of records into Redis in a short span by using Redis's protocol or pipelining functionality.

How to do it...

1. Pipelining makes it possible for clients to send several commands to Redis without waiting for the response, and then it starts waiting for the response from the server. The benefit of pipelining is to drastically increase the performance of communication. The performance improvement will increase approximately five times in case of faster connections and will lower in case of slow connections. The syntax for pipelining varies with the language libraries through which we are accessing Redis.

2. The following example shows how pipelining works in Ruby using the redis-rb (`https://github.com/redis/redis-rb`) client library. The code snippet assumes that Redis is running on the local machine and listening on the default port, 6379.

```
require "redis"
redis = Redis.new(:host => "127.0.0.1", :port => 6379)
redis.pipelined do
    redis.set "user", "user1"
    redis.set "userid", 1
    redis.incr "totallogin"
end
```

How it works...

Clients needing to write and update multiple keys as a response to some user action is a common operation. When multiple keys are to be updated, the commands are sent sequentially to Redis. Let us see how the commands are sent and how it affects performance. Assume that we need to write two new keys and increment a counter in Redis as a response to some user action. So there are three commands in total.

In this case, normally we need to perform three different operations:

```
SET user User1
OK
SET userid 1
OK
INCR totalLogin
(integer) 14
```

Considering a network roundtrip of 100 ms from the client to the server, and ignoring the Redis execution time, total time to execute all three commands will be:

Total time = (request sent + response from server) + (request sent + response from server) + (request sent+ response from server)

Total time = 100 ms + 100 ms + 100 ms (ignoring Redis's execution time)

Total time = 300 ms

So, the number of commands executed increases the time proportionally. This is because Redis is a TCP server running with request/response protocol. The server and the client are connected through a network socket and are forced to suffer the network latency even if you run the client on the server itself. Consider your Redis setup can process at least 50,000 requests per second, but if your network latency is 100 ms as described above, we can process only a maximum of 10 requests in a second, no matter how fast our Redis server works. As it is not possible to reduce the travel time between the server and client, the solution is to reduce the number of trips made between the server and client. In short, the lesser the number of round-trips, the more the number of requests processed by Redis in a second. Redis provides us with a solution for this problem: pipelining.

Let us take a look at the same example and see how pipelining will help us. As all the commands are sent to the server in a single flush over the wires, there will be only one roundtrip between the server and the client. So the time taken will be a little more than 100 ms. By using pipelining, we can gain a 200 percent performance increase for simple commands.

One thing to be aware of in pipelining is that the server will be forced to queue the response using the memory. So to prevent memory spikes, always send a considerable amount of commands in a single pipeline. We can send a few hundreds of commands, read the response, and then send another batch in the next pipeline to keep a check on memory usage. The performance will be almost the same.

By reducing the number of roundtrips between the server and the clients, pipelining provides an efficient way of writing data into Redis at faster speeds.

There's more...

There might be other situations where it is necessary to import millions of records into Redis in a very short span of time.

Bulk data import

The next type of data imports millions of records in a short span. In this recipe, we will take a look at how to feed Redis with a huge amount of data as fast as possible. Usually, bulk importing of data into Redis is performed in the following scenarios:

- When using Redis as a data store, bulk importing of data is done from relational databases such as MySQL

- When using the Redis server as a caching server, for prepopulating or warming the cache with most accessed caches

- Loading Redis with user-generated data or preexisting data

In these cases, the data to be imported is usually huge and has millions of writes. To achieve the import, using a normal Redis client is not a good idea as sending commands in a sequential manner will be slow and we need to pay for the roundtrip. We can use pipelining, but pipelining makes it impossible for the data inserted to be read at the same time, as Redis will not commit the data till all the commands in the pipeline are executed.

Redis protocol

The most recommended way to mass-import a huge data set is to generate a text file with the commands in the Redis protocol format and use the file to import the data into Redis. The redis-cli interface provides a pipe mode to perform a bulk import from a raw file with commands as per Redis protocol specifications (`http://redis.io/topics/protocol`).

The protocol is simple and binary safe, and its format is as follows:

```
*<number of arguments> CR LF
$<number of bytes of argument 1> CR LF
<argument data> CR LF
...
$<number of bytes of argument N> CR LF
<argument data> CR LF
```

Where `CR` is `\r` (or ASCII character 13) and `LF` is `\n` (or ASCII character 10).

For example, execute the following command:

```
SET samplekey testvalue
```

This command will look like the following in the raw file:

```
*3   - Number of arguments = SET + key + value = 3
$3   - Number of Bytes = 3 - SET has 3 bytes
SET
$8   - Number of bytes in samplekey
samplekey
$9
testvalue - Number of bytes in testvalue
```

This translates to the following:

```
*3\r\n$3\r\nSET\r\n$8\r\nsamplekey\r\n$9\r\ntestvalue\r\n
```

Redis uses the same format for both its request and response. As the protocol itself is simple, a simple program can generate a text file with all the commands in raw format.

Once the text file is generated, the data in the text file, say `redis-data.txt`, which has 1 million commands, can be imported into Redis using a simple command, as follows:

```
cat redis-data.txt | redis-cli --pipe
```

After the execution, the output will look like the following:

```
All data transferred. Waiting for the last reply...
Last reply received from server.
errors: 0, replies: 1000000
```

How does the pipe mode work?

The pipe mode not only tries to send the data to the server as fast as possible, but also reads and tries to parse the data when available. When it finds that there is no more data to send, it sends an `ECHO` command with a random 20 bytes to the server and then starts listening for the server's response. The server sends a response and sends the same 20 bytes to signal the end of the response. Because we use this, redis-cli does not need to know which commands or how many commands were sent to the server. But by counting the response, it provides us with a brief report about the status of our bulk import.

Leveraging data types (Simple)

One of the categories in which Redis stands out as a clear winner is its support for data types. Support for lists and sets makes it appropriate to call Redis an advanced data-store or data-structure server. It also provides very powerful and efficient atomic operations for manipulating data in these data structures. The official website of Redis provides extensive information about all the data structures available. But here we will discuss only a few important data structures and their use cases.

We have already discussed how to use the basic data structure, strings. Now we will see how to use lists, sets, and hashes. We will discuss each data structure in detail in the next section.

How to do it...

1. Open redis-cli or connect to the redis server through Telnet.
2. All the commands will be issued in redis-cli.
3. Let us create a list in Redis by using the following commands:

```
LPUSH greet "Hi"
(integer) 1
LPUSH greet "Redis"
(integer) 2
```

```
LRANGE greet 0 -1
1) "Hi"
2) "Redis"
LLEN greet
(integer) 2
```

4. Now let us have a look at how to use sets:

```
SADD set1 "1"
(integer) 1
SADD set1 "2"
(integer) 1
SADD set1 "3"
(integer) 1
SADD set2 "5"
(integer) 1
SADD set2 "3"
(integer) 1
SADD set2 "4"
(integer) 1
SUNION set1 set2
1) "2"
2) "3"
3) "5"
4) "1"
5) "4"
```

5. Hashes are more advanced data structures that open up lots of possibilities. Let us see how to use hashes:

```
HSET hash1 field1 "Hi"
(integer) 1
HSET hash1 field2 "Redis"
(integer) 1
HGETALL hash1
1) "field1"
2) "Hi"
3) "field2"
4) "Redis"
```

There's more...

We have seen how to use data structures. Now let us see where to use the data structures, and the different commands possible in each of them.

Strings

Strings are the most basic data type in Redis, implemented using a dynamic string library written in C. This basic type is binary safe and used to create more complex data types such as lists and sets. A string value can hold up to 512 MB of data. The string value can be anything from the HTML contents of a page to a binary stream of an image file.

There are many useful commands available to use on strings. A few notable ones are `INCR`, `DECR`, `INCRBY`, `SET`, `GET`, and `APPEND`.

 To know all the available commands in Redis, visit `http://redis.io/commands`.

Lists

Without the complex data types like lists and sets, Redis will be nothing but a MemCached server with persistence. In Redis, lists are nothing but a list of strings arranged based on the order of insertion. This ensures that the data can be accessed in the same order in which it was inserted. Internally, lists are implemented using **Linked List**, which has both pros and cons. The advantage is that adding an element in the head or tail of the list takes the same time. For example, adding an item to a list with 10 items or 10,000 items takes the same time, but the main disadvantage is that accessing an element in the middle of the list takes longer than accessing elements near the extremes. Being a database, it is critical to be able to add elements to a large list in an efficient way.

The `LPUSH` command is used to push new elements into the list and the `LLEN` command outputs the number of elements in the list.

 The lookup operation is $O(N)$, where N is the index of the element.

Various operations available for list manipulation make it easy to model queues or stacks. The maximum number of elements that can be stored in a list is $2^{32}-1$.

Sets

Redis sets are an unordered data collection of binary safe strings with no duplicate members. You should consider using sets when you have a collection of items and you need to add, delete, or verify the existence of members in a very efficient and fast manner. Another desired behavior is no duplication, and also support for peek and pop of elements (using the SRANDMEMBER and SPOP commands). Sets can also store up to 2^{32}-1 elements.

 Redis sets provide a constant time O(1) for all the mentioned operations, irrespective of the number of items you have in the set.

Sets also support complex operations like intersections and unions of members on the server side, which lets us perform transformations on the data before we get the output data. SADD is used to add an item into a set.

 Sets can be used to store indexes or inverted indexes, which are a critical part of any search system.

Sorted sets are introduced as a solution to a few shortcomings in sets, and are the most advanced data type in Redis. Similar to sets, sorted sets are also collections of non-repeating binary safe strings, but with a score associated to the member. The associated scores are used to sort the set from the smallest to the greatest score. We can add, delete, or update elements in a sorted set quickly, because elements are inserted in an order rather than ordered afterwards.

 Sorted sets achieve time complexity of O(log(N)).

Due to the highly optimized and efficient working of sorted sets, they can be used to maintain leader boards, timestamp range data, or to implement auto-completion with Redis. They make good priority queues and can be used to implement weighted random selections.

Hashes

Hashes are perfect to represent objects as a map between string fields and string values. Hashes are equivalent to a hash table or a hash map in Java. If we need to store some data related to an object and do not want to perform encoding (in JSON or XML, for example), hashes are the best suited. Hashes can be used to represent linked data structures using references.

 Complex data structures can be created using hashes, by creating a hash with a reference to lists and sets.

Optimizing memory (Intermediate)

Being a complete in-memory database, it is important to always have enough memory available for a Redis instance. As RAM is expensive in comparison to other resources, it is critical to optimize usage. In this recipe, we will see how we can optimize memory usage and how to prevent out-of-memory scenarios.

Getting ready

The memory can be used effectively by optimized design of the application, and also through server configurations. Redis provides a few transparent mechanisms to optimize memory usage. We can optimize the memory usage by following one or all the suggestions given in the next section. Few of these are inbuilt into Redis while others depend on the application requirements and design.

How to do it...

1. Implement CPU/memory tradeoffs. Configure the maximum number of elements and maximum element size for special encoding in the `6379.conf` file. Set the following variables:

   ```
   hash-max-zipmap-entries 64
   hash-max-zipmap-value 512
   list-max-ziplist-entries 512
   list-max-ziplist-value 64
   zset-max-ziplist-entries 128
   zset-max-ziplist-value 64
   set-max-intset-entries 512
   ```

2. Use hashes whenever possible. Maximize the usage of hashes, which along with the special encoding above will increase the performance.

3. Leverage auto-expiry of keys. Auto-expiry of volatile keys will help us to free memory automatically instead of waiting for an explicit key deletion. Set the expiry attribute to the keys using the following command:

   ```
   EXPIRE key Seconds
   ```

How it works...

In this section, let us discuss how the techniques in the previous section will help us use memory efficiently.

CPU/memory tradeoffs

We already discussed the special encoding used for small aggregate data types such as hashes, lists, sets, and sorted sets. The purpose of these encodings is to reduce the memory usage at the cost of CPU. These encodings are memory-efficient and take up to 10 times less memory. As soon as the size goes higher than the configured maximum size, the data set will be converted to normal encoding, which is completely transparent to the user.

Redis compiled with a 32-bit target leaves a lesser memory footprint compared to the 64-bit build, as the size of the pointer is small, but such an instance will be limited to 4 GB of maximum memory usage. The persistence files are compatible with both 32- and 64-bit instances and interchangeable without any trouble.

Maximize hash usage

Small hashes take less space in memory due to the special encoding discussed in the last section. So it is good to represent data in hashes whenever possible. For instance, if you want to store some data (ID, name, and price) for a product, use a single hash with all required fields instead of using different keys for each field. In this case, storing in a hash field will take three times less memory than storing the data as different keys.

For example, let us consider we want to cache small HTML fragments for our product catalog, in which the product ID ranges from 1,000 to 10,000. To store the fragments, we can use simple keys, with product ID as the key and the fragment as the value.

```
SET "Product:1000" "HTML snippet for 1000"
SET "Product:1001" "HTML snippet for 1001"
SET "Product:9875" "HTML snippet for 9875"
```

By using this method, we will end up creating 9,000 records in Redis. But we can save the same records as hash and save significant memory. Let us see how we can do that.

Every time we perform a SET operation, we will split the key into two parts. The first part will be used as the key and the second part as the hash field. In our case, the key name, Product:1000, will be split as key name Product:10 and field name 00. We will use the following command to set it:

```
HSET Product:10 00 "HTML snippet for 1000"
```

After adding all 9,000 items, the hash Product:10 will have a maximum of 100 fields and a maximum of 90 hashes in total, such as Product:11 and Product:12. By doing this, we have only 90 hash keys, each having 100 fields. This is a form of implicit presharding of keys. You can even save memory by keeping the key names short. For example, using pdt:10 is more efficient than using product:10.

If you are planning to store more than 100 fields in a hash, to take advantage of memory optimization, make sure the number is less than the value configured in `6379.conf`.

```
hash-max-zipmap-entries 256
```

```
hash-max-zipmap-value 1024
```

Caution

Once the limit is crossed, the data set will be converted to normal encoding and the memory saving will be lost.

The memory saving achieved using this method is phenomenal, making Redis the most memory-efficient data store. When benchmarking with a proper HTML snippet and 9,000 products, the result of memory usage is as follows:

▶ When stored as key-value pair, memory used was around 8.3 MB

▶ When optimized using hashes, memory used was around 1.1 MB

Auto expiry

Auto expiry is used to delete a key after a certain time. We can set a timeout on a key using the `EXPIRE` command. The error in the expiry is 0 to 1 millisecond in the latest Redis build (Version 2.6). The command is:

```
EXPIRE key Seconds
```

After the timeout, the key gets deleted automatically. Such keys are called **volatile keys** in Redis. The timeout can be cleared using the `SET` or `GETSET` commands. A volatile key can be made persistent using the `PERSIST` command. All other commands such as `INCR` or `HSET`, which do not replace the value, will leave the timeout intact. If a key gets renamed using the `RENAME` command, the timeout is also transferred to the new key name.

The expiry information of the keys is stored in UNIX time and it is heavily dependent on the computer clock. This makes sure the time flows even when Redis is not running.

Caution

While moving the RDB file between two computers, the time desync between the two computers can affect the expiration.

Internally, Redis performs expirations in two ways, passive and active. In the passive method, the expired key gets deleted when accessed by the client. This is not perfect as the expired keys that are never accessed will keep using memory. In the active mode, Redis performs sampling of 100 records per second and deletes all the expired keys. If the sampling results have more than 25 percent expired keys, the process continues.

There's more...

If you are planning to use Redis as a smarter MemCached replacement or purely as a caching server, this section provides more information on how we can use memory efficiently to accomplish that. Let us note what a simple caching system should support:

▸ Faster access to the cache data

▸ Auto-expiration of old caches

▸ Easier invalidation of caches, which is critical for any caching system

▸ Should use minimum resources and have the ability to control the amount of resources

Auto-expiring caching system

Let us discuss how Redis can serve as a perfect caching server, meeting all the basic requirements mentioned previously, in the case of caching an HTML page of the product catalog. The catalog has two types of pages, list pages and product-information pages.

As we have already seen, Redis is ultrafast, having the ability to serve more than 10,000 requests per second with no trouble, when deployed in entry-level servers.

In a typical system, a process checks Redis for a valid cache. If available, it delivers the cached HTML data to the client. If not available in Redis, the process generates the HTML and adds it to Redis as a cache to serve future requests efficiently. The cache needs to be refreshed periodically with fresh data. In this case, the auto-expiry feature in Redis comes in handy. Let us assume that our pricing data is valid for a maximum of three hours. Then, we can set the expiry for the product pages and list pages to three hours (10,800 seconds). This ensures that our cache gets refreshed every three hours.

The most common challenge to any caching system is **cache invalidation** and invalidating all dependencies. Taking our previous example, we have got a new price for only one product and now both the list page and the particular product page become invalid. It is critical to invalidate the cache before the expiry happens. It is unwise to invalidate the whole cache and recreate them. We need to invalidate only the cache of pages dependent on the changed product. For this purpose, Redis sets can be used to keep track of dependencies and only the dependent cache data need be expired.

Redis stores the cache in the memory. If we have millions of products in our catalog, we do not want to buy and install RAM to support our whole catalog. We want to limit the memory used while removing the least accessed cache to make space for new caches. Redis provides a simple solution to this problem. We can control the maximum memory Redis can use for its data through `/etc/redis/6379.conf`.

```
maxmemory <<bytes>>
```

If you have limited memory but would like to store more records, use hashes as described in the last section.

Other parameters can be used to specify the algorithm to be used to reclaim the memory. The following are as per the Redis documentation:

▶ **volatile-lru**: This removes a key among the ones with an expire set, trying to remove keys not recently used.

▶ **volatile-ttl**: This removes a key among the ones with an expire set, trying to remove keys with little time to live.

▶ **volatile-random**: This removes a random key among the ones with an expire set

▶ **allkeys-lru**: This parameter is like volatile-lru but will remove all kinds of keys, both normal keys or keys with an expire set

▶ **allkeys-random**: This parameter is like volatile-random but will remove all kinds of keys, both normal keys and keys with an expire set

For our example, volatile-lru makes sense as it will delete the keys with an expiry set and are the least recently used. This way we can limit the amount of memory used by Redis when used as a caching server.

Using transactions and Pub/Sub (Advanced)

In this section, let us discuss about a couple of important and advanced concepts in Redis, transactions and Publish/Subscribe. Transaction makes a series of commands to be executed atomically. Publish/Subscribe, shortly known as Pub/Sub, helps in **Inter-Process Communication** (**IPC**) by decoupling the two processes using Redis as a shared data queue. Let us discuss both topics in detail and an example for a Publish/Subscribe queue.

Pub/Sub implements the messaging paradigm, which makes it easy to detach two processes. Instead of a process sending messages to receivers, the messages are published to a channel with no knowledge about the subscribers who use it. In the same way, subscribers can subscribe to any number of channels showing their interest, for the message has no knowledge about the publisher. Using the simple Pub/Sub service in Redis, we can achieve high scalability.

How to do it...

First, let us see how to use transactions in Redis followed by Publish/Subscribe.

Transactions

1. The transaction is achieved using the `MULTI/EXEC` block.

2. The client uses the `MULTI` command to initiate a transaction, followed by all the other commands. Any command sent after `MULTI` will return the string `QUEUED`.

3. All the commands are queued and executed once the `EXEC` command is issued.

4. In this case, `MULTI` just starts the command queuing and `EXEC` is responsible for executing the operations. We can exit the transaction by calling the `DISCARD` function, which will flush out all the commands in the transaction queue. Let us see an example of a transaction executed in redis-cli.

```
redis> MULTI
OK
redis> SET key 10
QUEUED
redis> INCR key
QUEUED
redis> INCR key
QUEUED
redis>EXEC
1. OK
2. (integer) 11
3. (integer) 12
```

Publish/Subscribe

1. A process subscribes to any channel in Redis using the `SUBSCRIBE` command.

2. Another process can publish a message to the mentioned channel in Redis using the `PUBLISH` command.

3. The first process receives the published message from Redis and is free to process the message the way it wants.

4. At any point of time, the process can unsubscribe from a channel using the `UNSUBSCRIBE` command.

How it works...

Every command in Redis is atomic in nature and a transaction makes a series of commands to be executed atomically. All the commands are executed serially. As Redis is single-threaded and can process only one request at a time, it is not possible for commands issued by another client to be executed while a transaction is under execution. This provides the required isolation.

Transactions might sound familiar to pipelining, even those in which the commands are queued. But the difference is that the queue is maintained at the server for transactions, while pipelining is by clients.

The Pub/Sub feature does not involve any key/value storage but lets Redis act as a broadcast server that connects between the publishers and subscribers in real time. This makes Redis a good fit to implement modern web applications, such as chatting systems, messaging platforms, and notification systems.

There's more...

Let us discuss an example of how to use the Publish/Subscribe functionality in Redis.

A Publish/Subscribe example

Let us take the example where we are trying to implement a notification system in which we show a notification on receiving a new e-mail, on receiving a chat message, and if someone adds you as a friend. We have three processes working on these three functionalities. Our notification system needs to subscribe to all the three channels and show notifications.

To subscribe to a particular channel, the SUBSCRIBE command should be used if we know the channel name. In this case, our notification client will issue a subscription to all three channels.

```
SUBSCRIBE email chat addfriend
```

 If you want to subscribe to all channels matching a pattern, use PSUBSCRIBE instead. Find more information at http://redis.io/topics/pubsub.

Once subscribed to any channel, the client cannot issue any other commands but has to wait and read the stream of messages coming back from the server. There are three types of messages possible, which are identified by the first element of the message:

- ▶ SUBSCRIBE: This message is sent by the server to the clients to confirm the subscription, along with the total number of channels we have subscribed to.

- ▶ UNSUBSCRIBE: This message is to acknowledge the successful unsubscription from the server. This also contains the total number of channels we have active subscription to, as a third parameter.

- ▶ MESSAGE: This is the actual message published by the other clients. The second parameter has the channel name and the third parameter is the actual message.

For our command, the response will look something like this:

```
SUBSCRIBE email chat addfriend
*3
$9
subscribe
$5
first
:1
*3
$9
subscribe
$4
chat
:2
*3
$9
subscribe
$9
addfriend
:3
```

The format is the same as the Redis protocol, where the first line defines the number of arguments, followed by the number of bytes in arguments, and then the data itself. This confirms our subscription to all three channels. If we publish a message to any of the channels from another redis-cli, we use the PUBLISH command in the following manner:

```
PUBLISH chat Hi
```

Our notification client will receive the message stream as follows:

```
*3
$7
message
$4
chat
$2
Hi
```

Let us consider a case in which we want to give a provision to the user to stop notifications for chats when busy. In this case, it is possible to unsubscribe from a specific channel by using the UNSUBSCRIBE command.

```
UNSUBSCRIBE chat
*3
$11
unsubscribe
$4
chat
:2
```

The reply from the server will confirm the unsubscription, and also mentions that we have two remaining active subscriptions. Due to the simplicity of the Publish/Subscribe functionality, it is very easy to implement.

Caveats in transaction

Redis does not support rollbacks, which is an odd behavior when compared to other relational databases. So, even when an error occurs, Redis continues to execute the other commands. The rollbacking ability was sacrificed to keep the internal design simple and to keep Redis running fast. Another reason for not supporting rollbacks is that errors in Redis commands are only possible because of programming errors.

But there is a caveat. Due to the sequential manner of Redis's command execution in a transaction, it is not possible to perform a read operation during the transaction. Let us consider a case in which we want to write data into Redis based on the value in another key.

```
val = GET key1
MULTI
if val > 20:
    SET key2 (val+1)
EXEC
```

In this case, let us assume the value in `key1` was changed (value more than 20) after we read it and before the `EXEC` was executed. We will end up setting a wrong value to `key2`. Redis supports **Check and Set** (**CAS**) transactions to mitigate this issue. To use CAS, we need to use the `WATCH` command. The `WATCH` command provides a form of locking called Optimistic Locking, which is powerful.

```
WATCH key1
val = GET key1
MULTI
if val > 20:
    SET key2 (val+1)
EXEC
```

In this case, if the value of `key1` changes after the `WATCH` statement and before the `EXEC` command is executed, the transaction will fail. The client needs to retry again. The `WATCH` command can be called multiple times to watch multiple keys, or `WATCH` is called with multiple keys. The `WATCH` list is cleared once `EXEC` or `UNWATCH` is called.

 You can combine transactions with pipelining to perform faster atomic operations.

Troubleshooting and monitoring (Intermediate)

The computing world is not ideal and it is common to face issues and performance problems in Redis, which require troubleshooting techniques. In this section, let us discuss about commands that help in debugging and also about how to troubleshoot memory issues in Redis.

Redis is a simple piece of software that does not require complex debugging tools to identify the issues. Most of the time the issues in Redis are either due to wrong configuration or bad application design.

We have a couple of tools inbuilt into Redis that can help us identify what is really going on inside Redis. Let us see how to use the `monitor` command.

 Warning

The `monitor` command adds a lot of overhead to the server and should be used strictly for debugging, and as rarely as possible. The command can reduce the performance of the server significantly.

How to do it...

1. The `monitor` command, like any other command, issues through redis-cli or Telnet. So open redis-cli or Telnet to connect to Redis.

2. This command streams every command issued to the Redis server back to the client, which helps us to see what our server is going through.

3. Issue the following command:

   redis-cli monitor

4. After you issue this command, open another redis-cli and issue the following command:

   SET Google Android

5. In our monitor's command-line interface, we can see this command as follows:

   1356217734.180621 [0 127.0.0.1:62544] "set" "Google" "Android"

6. To stop the `monitor` command in redis-cli, you need to use *Ctrl + C* (SIGINT). The `monitor` command can be used by clients connected through Telnet too, in which case the `QUIT` command needs to be used to stop the command.

There's more...

A software without bugs does not exist. There might be situations when Redis does not behave as it should. Redis has got a solution to provide as much information as possible to the developers to fix the issues.

Slow log

The Redis Slow log is a system to log queries. The `slowlog` command is used to view the commands that exceeded the configured time in our configuration file. This command points out the queries that are running slowly, which can help us design the system better. Using this command, we can read the slow queries and also reset the queue. The Slow log is stored strictly in the memory, and provides quite rapid logging with little to no performance hit at the cost of extra memory to store the log.

To get the current length of the Slow log, use `slowlog len`. To read the Slow log, the `slowlog get` command should be used. This command returns the complete contents of the log. If you want only the latest N number of entries, pass the number to the command as follows:

```
slowlog get 2
```

The output format for the log will be:

```
1)1) (integer) 7
    2) (integer) 1356248799
    3) 15
    4)  1) "SUNIONSTORE"
        2) "Set1"
        3) "set2"
        4) "set3"
2) 1) (integer) 6
    2) (integer) 1356248815
    3) 12
    4)  1) "SINTER"
        2) "Set1"
        3) "set2"
        4) "set3"
```

The preceding log output has two entries. Every entry consists of four fields, as follows:

▸ A unique auto-incrementing identifier for every log. The identifier will be reset on server restart.

▸ The Unix timestamp at which the logged command was executed.

▸ The amount of time needed for its execution, in microseconds.

▸ The arguments of the command in the form of an array.

To reset the Slow log, use the `slowlog reset` command. Once the command is executed, the log information is lost forever.

Redis software watchdog

In the latest version (v2.6.13) of Redis, a new debugging tool for developers has been introduced, watchdog. It is designed to track latency problems that could escape analysis using normal tools. This feature is still experimental and should be used in production with caution as a last resort when all other means of debugging fail. It is not advisable to keep the watchdog running for an extended period of time. The output is logged into a logfile that contains low-level reports about the server component. The log can be sent to the Redis community to figure out what caused the block in the server and fix the problem, if any, in the server.

Caution

Be sure to switch off the watchdog by using the command `CONFIG SET watchdog-period 0`.

To enable the watchdog, you need to use the `CONFIG SET` command as follows:

```
CONFIG SET watchdog-period 700
```

The preceding command will log any latency issues if the delay is more than 700 milliseconds. The minimum time that can be mentioned is 200 milliseconds.

Using languages and drivers (Simple)

All the major programming languages have support for Redis through their client libraries. Even if your language of preference does not have a client library to connect and use Redis, it is fairly easy to write a basic client of your own, as the Redis protocol is simple to implement. So, in this recipe, we will cover some clients worth mentioning for commonly used programming languages.

 It is important to update the client libraries when we update the Redis server to get support for new commands and features.

Let us see how to use client libraries to connect to Redis. As part of this recipe, we will see how we can use redis-rb to connect to Redis using Ruby.

How to do it...

1. You need to download the redis-rb client library from the official GitHub page (`https://github.com/redis/redis-rb`).

2. Create a new Ruby script that will connect to the Redis server. The following code should make a connection to the server, assuming the server is running on the local machine at port 6379:

   ```
   require "redis"
   redis = Redis.new(:host => "127.0.0.1", :port => 6379)
   ```

3. After connecting, we can execute the following commands:

   ```
   redis.set("redis", "rocks")
   redis.get('redis')
   ```

4. Close the connection once done.

   ```
   redis.quit
   ```

There's more...

You can find multiple libraries that provide almost similar functionalities; the complete list of libraries available for Redis can be found on the official Redis website (`http://redis.io/clients`). Here we were focusing on stable, active, recommended, and feature-complete libraries only. An official supported library is available only for C; all the libraries for other languages were written and are maintained by the community or external developers.

Client Libraries

The following table has the recommended libraries for popular programming languages (which are stable enough to be used in production):

Languages	Library Name	Repository URL
C	hiredis (Officially supported)	`https://github.com/redis/hiredis`
PHP	Predis	`https://github.com/nrk/predis`
Ruby	redis-rb	`https://github.com/redis/redis-rb`
Perl	Redis	`https://github.com/melo/perl-redis`
Python	redis-py	`https://github.com/andymccurdy/redis-py`
Java	Jedis	`https://github.com/xetorthio/jedis`
Node.js	node_redis	`https://github.com/mranney/node_redis`
Objective-C	ObjCHiredis	`https://github.com/lp/ObjCHiredis`
C#	Booksleeve	`http://code.google.com/p/booksleeve/`

PUBLISHING

Spring Data

ISBN: 978-1-84951-904-5   Paperback: 160 pages

Implement JPA repositories with less code and harness the performance of Redis in your applications

1. Implement JPA repositories with lesser code

2. Includes functional sample projects that demonstrate the described concepts in action and help you start experimenting right away

3. Provides step-by-step instructions and a lot of code examples that are easy to follow and help you to get started from page one

Apache Solr 4 Cookbook

ISBN: 978-1-78216-132-5   Paperback: 328 pages

Over 100 recipes to make Apache Solr faster, more reliable, and return better results

1. Learn how to make Apache Solr search faster, more complete, and comprehensively scalable

2. Solve performance, setup, configuration, analysis, and query problems in no time

3. Get to grips with, and master, the new exciting features of Apache Solr 4

Please check **www.PacktPub.com** for information on our titles